D0730678

DETERMINED

The STORY of HOLOCAUST SURVIVOR
AVRAHAM PERLMUTTER

A. Avraham Perlmutter, Ph.D.

Mascherato
Publishing

Copyright © 2014 by A. Avraham Perlmutter, Ph.D.

All rights reserved.

No parts of this book may be used or reproduced without
permission of A. Avraham Perlmutter except in the case of brief
quotations in reviews for inclusion in a magazine, newspaper, broadcast,
or presentations of holocaust survivor histories.

ISBN: 193794509X
ISBN 13: 9781937945091

Library of Congress Control Number: 2014910900
Mascherato Publishing
P.O. Box 1550
Pacific Palisades, CA 90272
publishing@mascherato.com

CONTENTS

ACKNOWLEDGEMENTS

First and foremost, I would like to thank my lovely wife, Ruth, and our children, Michael, David, Sharon, and Keren, for their love and support, and for encouraging me to publish the story of my life. I am also grateful to Keren for gathering additional research, editing the book, and preparing it for publication.

I was fortunate to have survived the life-threatening dangers of the Holocaust and other experiences during the War of Independence of Israel. I hope that the story of my DETERMINATION will contribute to future generations being DETERMINED to achieve their dreams by overcoming any difficulties in their lives. I also was interviewed for Steven Spielberg's Shoah Visual History Foundation, which together with the stories of other survivors will provide historical information about the brutality of the Nazi regime.

I cannot thank enough all the brave and wonderful people in the Netherlands, who at terrible danger to themselves and their families saved my life by providing hiding places for me.

I appreciate the various organizations and people who provided me with additional information and documentation, including Michlean Amir at the United States Holocaust Memorial Museum and Miriam Keesing at the Dutch *Kindertransport* website dokin.nl.

I am also thankful for the beneficial editorial feedback from Laurel Hoctor-Jones and Jessica Keet, the helpful comments from Sharon Perlmutter Gavin, Michael Perlmutter, and Andy Gavin, and the excellent book cover design by James T. Egan at www.bookflydesign.com.

A. Avraham (Av) Perlmutter
Santa Monica, California
June 2014

PART 1

DETERMINED *to* SURVIVE

GRUBBENVORST, NETHERLANDS; NOVEMBER 25, 1944

Thunderous artillery explosions fired by the British army illuminated the night sky as I crawled on hands and knees on the road from Grubbenvorst to Sevenum. With my hands, I carefully checked the ground for mines planted by the Germans to impede the British advance. I inched toward the Allied lines less than a mile away, desperately trying to escape from the murderous Nazis.

Suddenly, I heard shouts of "Halt!" as several Nazi soldiers launched toward me from the side of the road. As I stood up, one of them grabbed my arm and demanded in German that I tell him who I was and where I was going.

A horrible thought flashed through my mind: *After years of dangerous escapes, so close to liberation, would this be my end?*